LEVEL
1

Amelia Earhart

Caroline Crosson Gilpin

NATIONAL
GEOGRAPHIC

Washington, D.C.

For Diane Crosson McEnroe

The publisher and author gratefully acknowledge the expert review of this book by Sammie L. Morris, university archivist and head, archives and special collections, Purdue University.

Trade paperback ISBN: 978-1-4263-1350-9
Reinforced library binding ISBN: 978-1-4263-1351-6

Book design by YAY! Design

Cover (portrait), Underwood & Underwood/Corbis; (airplane), AP Images; 1, Bettmann/Corbis; 2, The Granger Collection, NY; 4, Photo Researchers RM/Getty Images; 6, AP Images; 6, Washington Stock Photo/Alamy; 7, Bettmann/Corbis; 8, Photograph by Leslie Jones, courtesy of the Boston Public Library; 9, The Granger Collection, NY; 10, Private collection of Karsten Smedal, courtesy of Ames Historical Society; 11, Karnes Archives and Special Collections Research Center/Purdue University Libraries; 12 (top), PhotoQuest/Getty Images; 12 (bottom left), Dorling Kindersley/Getty Images; 12 (bottom right), Lawrence Manning/Corbis; 13 (top), NoDerog/iStockphoto; 13 (center), Car Culture/Getty Images; 13, Fox Photos/Hulton Archive/Getty Images; 15, The Granger Collection, NY; 16, Corbis; 16 (bottom), AFP/AFP/Getty Images/Newscom; 17, Bettmann/Corbis; 18, Orhan Cam/Shutterstock; 19 (top), AP Images; 19, Pictures Inc./Time & Life Pictures/Getty Images; 20, Karnes Archives and Special Collections Research Center/Purdue University Libraries; 21, Bettmann/Corbis; 21, ZUMA Wire Service/Alamy; 22–23 (background), Konstantin L/Shutterstock; 22 (top left), Olyina/Shutterstock; 22 (top right), Victor Tyakht/Shutterstock; 22 (bottom), AP Images; 23 (top), Kumar Sriskandan/Alamy; 23 (bottom left), The Granger Collection, NY; 23 (bottom right), The Denver Post/Getty Images; 25, AP Images; 26, Ben Margot/AP Images; 26–27, EcOasis/Shutterstock; 27, AP Images; 28–29, EcOasis/Shutterstock; 29, Bettmann/Corbis; 30 (left), Ensuper/Shutterstock; 30 (right), AP Images; 31 (top left), Jami Garrison/Shutterstock; 31 (top right), Bettmann/Corbis; 31 (bottom left), DEA Picture Library/De Agostini/Getty Images; 31 (bottom right), Neftali/Shutterstock; 32 (top left), Diane Miller/Photolibrary RM/Getty Images; 32 (top right), The Granger Collection, NY; 32 (bottom left), AP Images; 32 (bottom right), Bettmann/Corbis

**National Geographic supports K–12 educators with ELA Common Core Resources.
Visit natgeoed.org/commoncore for more information.**

Printed in the United States of America
18/WOR/3

Table of Contents

Who Was Amelia Earhart?

Words to Know

PILOT: A person who flies an airplane

Airplanes were new in the 1920s. People mostly traveled by car or boat or train. But Amelia Earhart dreamed of flying.

Amelia was one of the first women pilots. She was known all over the world. She did many things women had never done before.

Growing Up

The house where Amelia was born

Amelia Mary Earhart was born on July 24, 1897.

She grew up in Atchison, Kansas.
She had a sister named Muriel.

The girls played football and fished.
They read books and collected bugs.

Back then girls wore long dresses.
But Amelia's mother made them
playsuits (PLAY-soots). Then they
could run and play like the boys.

In Her Own Words

"I believe that women have as much courage as men."

Amelia's family moved a lot.
She went to many different schools.
Amelia made friends easily.
She enjoyed making people laugh.

When Amelia grew up, she worked
as a nurse. Later, she worked at a
center that helped poor children.
The children loved her.

Amelia loved to help people.

Amelia in her nurse's uniform

A Love of Flying

When Amelia was 23, her father took her to an air show. She took a short ride in an airplane that day. Amelia fell in love with flying.

In Her Own Words

"As soon as we left the ground, I knew I myself had to fly."

Amelia with the first plane she owned

Amelia wanted to be a pilot.
She worked hard to earn money
for lessons.

Amelia's first teacher was pilot Neta Snook.

In Her Time

Many things were different in the late 1920s and 1930s.

Jobs

Most people did not have a lot of money. There were not many jobs.

Money

A stuffed teddy bear cost 98 cents.

Radio

People did not have TVs in their homes. Most people listened to the radio.

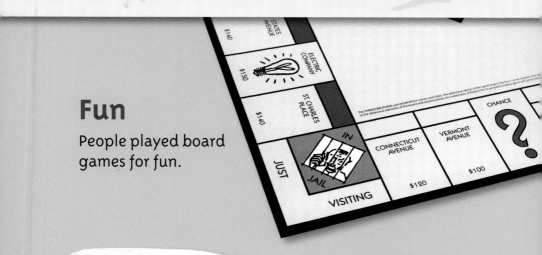

Fun

People played board games for fun.

Cars

Cars were much slower than they are today. They couldn't go very far, either.

Women

Finding jobs was harder for women than for men. Some people thought women shouldn't work outside the home.

Amelia always tried to do better. She flew fast. She flew high.

Amelia wanted to be the first woman pilot to cross the Atlantic Ocean. It was very dangerous. Many people had died trying.

But in 1932, she made the long, hard trip. And she did it! All by herself.

In Her Own Words

"Adventure is worthwhile
in itself."

Becoming Famous

Amelia Earhart was becoming famous. She was well known because she was a great pilot, but also because she was a woman pilot.

In Her Own Words

"Women must try to do things as men have tried."

Amelia taught women college students about jobs and careers.

Not many women had careers (kuh-REERS) in the 1930s. But Amelia did. She told women they could have careers, too.

Words to Know

CAREER: A person's life work

Amelia wrote books about her flying career. She gave speeches all over the country. In 1933, she was invited to the White House.

Amelia became friends with Eleanor Roosevelt, President Franklin Roosevelt's wife. She took Mrs. Roosevelt for a ride in her plane. Mrs. Roosevelt wished she could be a pilot, too.

The White House

Amelia and Eleanor Roosevelt agreed that women could do the same kinds of jobs as men.

An American Hero

Amelia got many awards and medals. She spoke to college students about aviation (ay-vee-AY-shun). People everywhere wanted to be like her.

Words to Know

AVIATION: The world of flying and airplanes

Amelia at Purdue University
(per-DOO YOO-nuh-VUR-suh-tee)

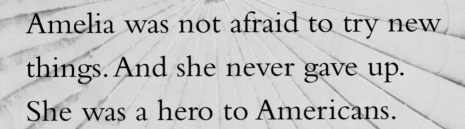

Amelia was not afraid to try new things. And she never gave up. She was a hero to Americans.

Amelia helped test a parachute (PAR-ruh-shoot).

Amelia was the first woman to get this medal. It is the U.S. Distinguished (dis-TING-gwisht) Flying Cross.

6 Fun Facts About Amelia

1

Amelia drank hot cocoa and ate oranges on her plane trips.

2

Pilots used to be called "aviators." The word comes from "avis." It means "bird" in Latin.

3

Amelia married George Putnam in 1931. He published books. He helped Amelia with her career.

4

One of Amelia's planes is at the Smithsonian (smith-SOWN-ee-un) National Air and Space Museum. It's in Washington, D.C.

5

Amelia was the first president of the Ninety-Nines. This is a group of women flyers.

6

Amelia had her own U.S. postage stamp! It came out in 1963.

Around the Globe

Amelia always dreamed of flying around the world. She got a bigger, faster plane to make the trip.

Amelia took Fred Noonan with her. He was her navigator (NAV-uh-gay-tur). His job was to give directions. Amelia's job was to fly the plane.

Words to Know

NAVIGATOR: A person who uses maps to help find the way

In Her Own Words

"Flying may not be all plain sailing, but the fun of it is worth the price."

The Last Flight

Amelia and Fred flew for one month. They flew across deserts and mountains. But the hard part was next. They had to fly over the huge Pacific Ocean (puh-SIF-ik OH-shun).

A Lockheed Electra 10E airplane, the same model Amelia used in her flight around the world

1897
Born July 24 in Atchison, Kansas

1916
Graduates from high school

1918
Works as a Red Cross nurse

The cockpit of Amelia's plane

They would have to stop for gas on a tiny island. It was hard to find. But Amelia was brave. On July 2, 1937, she took off from her final stop.

1921
Learns to fly from pilot Neta Snook. Buys her first airplane.

1922
Sets record for highest flying, at 14,000 feet

1926
Works at a children's center in Boston

Suddenly, the plane couldn't be reached by radio. No one is sure what happened. Many people believe the plane ran out of gas and crashed. Amelia was never found.

Amelia Earhart was a great pilot. She taught others to live without fear. She was loved by people all over the world.

1930
Sets record for fastest flying, at 181 miles an hour

1931
Marries book publisher George Putnam

1932
Flies across the Atlantic Ocean alone, landing in Ireland

Amelia's final flight

— where Amelia flew
● stops she made
not all stops are shown

ASIA

EUROPE

start

NORTH AMERICA

West Africa

AFRICA

Pakistan

California

Florida

Ethiopia

Thailand

New Guinea

Amelia disappears over Pacific Ocean

AUSTRALIA

Brazil

SOUTH AMERICA

1936

Purdue University gives Amelia money to buy a Lockheed Electra 10E airplane

1937

Sets off to fly around the world. Disappears July 2, 1937.

2012

New search begins for Amelia's plane. Nothing concrete found yet.

What in the World?

These pictures show close-up views of items from Amelia Earhart's time. Use the hints to figure out what's in the pictures. Answers are on page 31.

HINT: A machine used to fly

HINT: It protects your head.

WORD BANK

stamp   map   medal   airplane   goggles   helmet

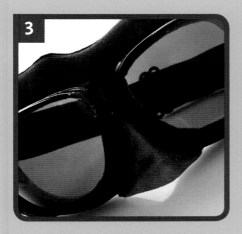

HINT: They cover your eyes.

HINT: An award

HINT: You can use this to find your way.

HINT: It goes on a piece of mail.

Answers: 1. airplane, 2. helmet, 3. goggles, 4. medal, 5. map, 6. stamp

AVIATION: The world of flying and airplanes

CAREER: A person's life work

NAVIGATOR: A person who uses maps to help find the way

PILOT: A person who flies an airplane